Published By Adam Gilbin

@ Brent Morin

Sirtfood Diet: Cooking Healthy Dishes and Losing

Weight Quickly With Basic Concepts Of The

Sirtfood Diet

All Right RESERVED

ISBN 978-87-94477-26-0

AF110312

TABLE OF CONTENTS

Green Laden Egg Scramble 1

Spicy Scramble 3

Green Omelet 5

Smoked Salmon Omelet 7

Baked Potatoes With Spicy Chickpea Stew 9

Chinese-Style Pork With Pack Choir 13

Chicken And Broccoli Curry With Potatoes Bombay 17

Spiced Scrambled Eggs 21

Chili Con Carne Sirt 23

Strawberry, Tomato & Watercress Salad With Honey & Pink Pepper Dressing 26

Soy Salmon & Broccoli Traybake 28

Turmeric Salmon 30

Waldorf Salad 33

Bacon Roasted Brussel Sprouts 35

Maple Roasted Acorn Squash With Cornbread Stuffing 38

Lamb, Butternut Squash And Date Tagine 42

Prawn Arrabbiata 46

Beans With Beef 50

Chargrilled Beef, A Red Wine Jus, Onion Rings, Garlic Kale, And Herb Roasted Potatoes 53

Black Bean Salsa 56

Buckwheat Pasta Salad 58

Greek Salad Skewers 60

Mushroom Dip 63

Choc Chip Granola-Sirtfood Recipes 64

Fragrant Asian Hotpot-Sirtfood 67

Buckwheat Noodles With Chicken Kale & Miso 70

Prawn Stir-Fry With Buckwheat 74

Buckwheat Groats With Banana And Chocolate Topping 78

Overnight Oats With Banana And Peanut Butter 80

Overnight Oats With Chocolate And Figs 82

Wholesome Buckwheat Granola 84

Cinnamon Buckwheat And Walnuts 86

Pancakes With Apples And Blackcurrants 87

Granola 91

Tuscan Bean Stew 93

Kale And Red Onion Dhal With Buckwheat 96

Char Grilled Beef With Onion Rings, Garlic Kale And Herb Roasted Potatoes. 98

Scramble Mushroom And Tofu 103

Salmon Pasta Smoked With Chili And Arugula 105

Soba Noodles In Miso Broth With Tofu, Celery And Kale 108

Tuscan-Style Bean Stew 110

Turmeric Baked Salmon 113

Buckwheat With Mushrooms And Green Onions 116

Turmeric Chicken & Kale Salad With H2y Lime Dressing-Sirtfood Recipes 117

Chicken Breasts 121

Sweet Potato Breakfast 124

French Toast With Apple Sauce 126

Veggie Omelet 128

Main Meals Recipe 129

Salmon & Capers 132

Moroccan Chicken Casserole 134

Sesame Dip 137

Salsa Bean Dip 138

Green Laden Egg Scramble

Ingredients:

- 1 teaspoon fresh basil, chopped
- 1 teaspoon fresh parsley, chopped
- 1 tablespoon olive oil
- 2 eggs, whisked
- 25 grams 1 ounce rocket arugula leaves
- 1 teaspoon chives, chopped

Directions:

1. Mix the eggs with the rocket arugula and herbs.
2. Heat the oil in a frying pan and pour it into the egg mixture.

3. Gently stir until it's lightly scrambled.
4. Season and serve.

Spicy Scramble

Ingredients:

- 1 teaspoon turmeric
- 1 tablespoon olive oil
- Sea salt to taste
- 25 grams 1 ounce kale, finely chopped
- 2 eggs
- 1 spring onion scallion finely chopped
- Freshly ground black pepper to taste

Directions:

1. Crack the eggs into a bowl.
2. Add the turmeric and whisk them.

3. Season with salt and pepper.
4. Heat the oil in a frying pan, add the kale and spring onions scallions and cook until it has wilted.
5. Pour in the beaten eggs and stir until eggs have scrambled together with the kale.

Green Omelet

Ingredients:

- Handful arugula
- 3 sprigs of parsley, chopped
- 1 tsp. extra virgin olive oil
- 1 shallot, peeled and chopped
- Salt and black pepper

Directions:

1. Beat the eggs in a small bowl and set aside.
2. Sauté the shallot for 5 minutes with a bit of the oil, on low-medium heat.
3. Pour the eggs in the pans, stirring the mixture for just a second.

4. The eggs on a medium heat, and tip the pan just enough to let the loose egg run underneath after about 2 minute on the burner.
5. Add the greens, herbs, and the seasonings to the top side as it is still soft.
6. TIP: You do not even have to flip it, as you can just cook the egg slowly egg as is well.
7. TIP: Another option is to put it into an oven to broil for 3-5 minutes checking to make sure it is only until it is golden but burned.

Smoked Salmon Omelet

Ingredients:

- ½ teaspoon of capers
- 2 medium eggs
- 1 teaspoon of chopped Parsley
- 10g of chopped Rocket
- 100g smoked salmon, sliced
- 1 teaspoon of extra virgin olive oil

Directions:

1. Crack the eggs into a bowl and whisk them well.

2. Add the capers, parsley, rocket, and salmon and heat oil in a non-stick pan until hot but not smoking.
3. Add the egg mixture into the pan and move it around the pan using a spatula.
4. Reduce the heat to low and let the omelet cook.
5. Slide the spatula under the omelet, fold it up in half, and serve.

Baked Potatoes With Spicy Chickpea Stew

Ingredients::

- 2 x 14-ounce tins cleaved tomatoes

- 1 ounce unsweetened cocoa powder or cacao

- 2 x 14-ounce tins chickpeas or kidney beans assuming you like including the chickpea water DON'T DRAIN!!

- 3 yellow peppers or whatever shading you like!, hacked into scaled down pieces

- 1 ounce parsley in addition to extra for decorate Salt and pepper to taste discretionary Side serving of mixed

- greens optional 4-6 baking potatoes, pricked all over

- 1 ounces olive oil

- Four cloves garlic, ground or squashed

- 2cm ginger, grated

- 3 red onions, finely chopped

- ½ - 2 teaspoons stew drops contingent upon how hot you like
  things 1 ounce cumin seeds

- 2 tablespoons turmeric Splash of water

Directions:

1. Preheat the stove to 390°F while you can set up every 2 of the provisions you need.
2. Put your baking potatoes in the broiler when the broiler is adequately hot, and cook them

for 1 hour or until as long as they are d2 as you like them.
3. Add the olive oil and slashed red onion in an enormous wide pot once the potatoes are in the stove and cook tenderly with the cover until the onions are delicate however not brown for 5 minutes.
4. Remove the top and add the garlic, cumin, ginger, and Chili.
5. Cook on low heat for another minute, then add the turmeric and a few drops of water and cook for another minute, being careful not to let the saucepan get too hot.
6. Add cocoa or cacao powder, chickpeas counting chickpea water, and yellow pepper in the tomatoes. Put to bubble and cook for 45 minutes at low hotness until the sauce is weighty and unctuous however don't allow it to consume!.

7. The stew ought to be taken care of simultaneously as the potatoes.
8. At last, mix in the 1 ounce of parsley and some salt and pepper, whenever wanted, and serve the stew over the heated potatoes, maybe with a basic side salad.

Chinese-Style Pork With Pack Choir

Ingredients:

- 0.5 ounce rice wine

- 0.5 ounce tomato pure

- 0.166 ounce brown sugar

- 0.5 ounce soy sauce

- 2 clove garlic, stripped and crushed

- 2 thumb 5cm new ginger, stripped and ground
  0.5 ounce rapeseed oil

- 3.52 ounce shiitake mushrooms, cut

- 14 ounce firm tofu, cut into enormous cubes

- 0.5 ounce corn flour
- 0.5 ounce water
- 125ml chicken stock
- 2 shallot, stripped and sliced
- Take 7.05 ounce pak choi or Choi aggregate, cut into slight cuts 14 ounce pork mince 10% fat
- 3.52 ounce bean sprouts
- Large modest bunch 0.70 ounce parsley, chopped.

Directions:

1. Put the Tofu on paper for the kitchen, cover with more paper for the kitchen, and set aside.

2. Mix the water and corn flour together in a little bowl, eliminating every 2 of the protuberances.
3. Add the chicken stock, rice wine, purée tomatoes, earthy colored sugar, and sauce soya. Attach the smashed garlic and ginger, then mix.
4. Add oil and hotness to a high temperature in a wok or wide griddle. Attach the shiitake mushrooms, then stir-fry until cooked, then shiny for 23 minutes.
5. Yake mushrooms out pf the container and set to the side with an opened spoon. Connect the Tofu to the pan and sautéed food the 3 sides until brilliant. Eliminate with a spoon and set aside.
6. Add the shallot and Choi mixture to the wok, stir-fry for 2 minutes, then apply the thinner.
7. Cook until the slim is cooked through, then add the sauce, reduce a notch of heat. Join

the beansprouts, mushrooms shiitake, and Tofu to the pan and concoct. Eliminate from oil, race in the parsley, and quickly serve.

Chicken And Broccoli Curry With Potatoes Bombay

Ingredients:

- Chopped tomatoes 1 x 14-ounce 400 g

- Chicken stock: 21/8 cups 500ml

- 7/8 cup coconut milk 200ml

- 2 tops of cardamom

- 1 stick of cinnamon

- 11/3 lbs 600 g of russet potatoes

- 1/4 cup 10 g chopped parsley

- 22/3 cups 175 g, sliced kale

- 4 x 41/2- to 51/2-ounce 120-150 g skinless chicken breasts, cut into pieces of bite size

- 4 spoonfuls of extra virgin olive oil

- 3 tablespoons of turmeric soil

- 2 red, sliced onions

- 2 thai, finely chopped chilies

- 4 cloves of garlic, finely chopped

- 1 tablespoon of new ginger, finely chopped

- 1 table litre of mild curry powder

- 2 tablespoons 5 g of chopped coriander

Directions:

1. Rub the pieces of chicken in 1 teaspoon of oil, and 1 tablespoon of turmeric. Hang on for 30 minutes to marinate.
2. Fry the chicken over high heat the chicken should be fried with ample oil in the marinade for 4 to 5 minutes until well browned all over and fried through, then remove from the pan and set aside.
3. Heat 1 spoonful of the oil over medium heat in the frying pan and add the onion, chili, garlic and ginger.
4. Fry for about 10 minutes or until tender, then add the curry powder and another turmeric tablespoon and cook for 1 to 2 minutes.
5. Add the tomatoes to the pan and allow to cook for another 2 minutes. Remove the stock, coconut milk, cardamom and cinnamon stick and leave for 45 to 60 minutes to simmer.

6. Check the pan frequently to ensure it doesn't run dry — you may need to add more storage.
7. Heat the frying pan to 425 ° F 220 ° C. Peel the potatoes while your curry is cooking, and cut them into small chunks.
8. Place the remaining tablespoon of turmeric in boiling water, and boil for 5 minutes.
9. Drain well, and prepare for 10 minutes of dry steam. Round the edges they should be white and flaky.
10. Transfer to a roasting pan, stir in the remaining oil and roast until golden brown and crisp for 30 minutes. When they are ready, throw the parsley through.
11. Add the kale, cooked chicken, and coriander when the curry has your required consistency, and cook for another 5 minutes to ensure the chicken is cooked through, then serve with the potatoes.

Spiced Scrambled Eggs

Ingredients:

- 1/2 Thai pepper, finely chopped

- 3 Medium-sized Eggs

- 1/4 cup milk 50ml

- 1 Teaspoon of turmeric powder

- 1 cup of extra virgin olive oil

- 1/8 cup 20 g red, finely chopped onion

- 2 Table cubits 5 g of parsley, finely chopped

Directions:

1. In a frying pan, heat the oil and fry the red onion and chili until soft but not brown.

2. Whisk the eggs, the milk, the turmeric and the parsley together.
3. Add to the hot pan and continue to cook over low to medium heat, moving the egg mixture around the pan constantly to scramble it and stop it from sticking / burning.
4. Serve when you have achieved the consistency you desire.

Chili Con Carne Sirt

Ingredients:

- 1 Red bell potato, cored, seeds removed and cut into bits of bite size
- Chopped tomatoes 2 x 14-ounce 400 g cans
- 1 Tomato cubit purée
- 1 Table litre of cocoa powder
- 7/8 cup 150 g of frozen reindeer
- Beef stock: 11/4 cups 300ml
- 2 Tablespoons 5 g fresh, chopped coriander
- 2 Tablespoons 5 g of fresh, chopped parsley
- 1 Red, finely chopped onion

- 4 cloves of garlic, finely chopped

- 2 Thai, finely chopped chilies

- 1 litre, extra virgin olive oil

- 1 Tablespoon cumin in the ground

- 1 Tablespoon of turmeric soil

- Lean beef 5 per cent fat 1 pound 450 g

- Red wine: 5/8 cup 150ml

- 1 Cup Buckwheat 160 g

Directions:

1. Fry the onion, garlic, and chili in the oil for 2 to 3 minutes over medium heat in a large saucepan, then add the spices and cook for another minute or 3.

2. Add the ground beef and cook over medium-high heat for 2 to 3 minutes until the meat is well browned throughout.
3. Add the red wine, and allow it to bubble to halve it.
4. Add the red pepper, tomatoes, purée tomatoes, cocoa, kidney beans and stock and leave for 1 hour to simmer.
5. Occasionally, you would need to apply a little water to maintain a dense, sticky consistency. Stir in the chopped herbs, just before serving.
6. Meanwhile, according to the package instructions, cook the buckwheat and serve alongside the chili.

Strawberry, Tomato & Watercress Salad With Honey & Pink Pepper Dressing

Ingredients:

- 300g strawberries

- 250g mixed tomatoes

- 100g watercress, woody stalks discarded

For the dressing

- ½ lemon, juiced

- 3 tbsp extra virgin olive oil

- 1 tbsp pink peppercorns

- 2 strawberries about 40g, chopped

- ½ tbsp honey

Directions:

1. For the dressing, toast the peppercorns in a dry frying pan for 1-2 mins until fragrant, then bash briefly using a pestle and mortar with a pinch of salt to break up the skins. Add the 2 strawberries and smash them to a paste.
2. Stir in the h2y and lemon juice. Tip the dressing into a large bowl, and whisk in the olive oil.
3. Check for seasoning, then add a little more salt or lemon juice, if you like.
4. To assemble the salad, cut the strawberries into quarters or slim wedges, and roughly chop the tomatoes, slicing some and halving others so you get lots of different shapes. Mix with the watercress in the bowl.
5. Divide the salad between four plates or pile onto a platter. Spoon over any dressing left in the bowl.

Soy Salmon & Broccoli Traybake

Ingredients:

- juice ½ lemon , ½ lemon quartered

- small bunch spring onions , sliced

- 2 tbsp soy sauce

- 4 skin-on salmon fillets

- 1 head broccoli , broken into florets

Directions:

1. Preheat oven, Put the salmon in a large roasting tin, leaving space between each fillet.
2. Wash and drain the broccoli and, while still a little wet, arrange in the tray around the fillets. Pour the lemon juice over everything, then add the lemon quarters.

3. Top with half the spring onions, drizzle with a little olive oil and put in the oven for 14 mins.
4. Remove from the oven, sprinkle everything with the soy, then return to the oven for 4 mins more until the salmon is cooked through. Sprinkle with the remaining spring onions just before serving.

Turmeric Salmon

Ingredients:

- 1 clove of garlic, finely chopped or pressed
- 1 Bire's Eye Chili, finely chopped
- 150g celery, cut into 2cm long pieces
- 1 teaspoon mild curry powder
- 130g tomato, cut into pieces
- 100ml chicken or vegetable stock
- 1 tbsp chopped parsley
- Skin salmon
- 1 teaspoon of virgin olive oil

- 1 teaspoon ground turmeric

- ¼ lemon juice

- 1 teaspoon of virgin olive oil

- 40g red onion, finely chopped

- 60g tinned green lentils

Directions:

1. First, we preheat the oven to 200 ° C or gas level.
2. Now we can start preparing. Now the celery pieces, the olive oil, the onion, the garlic and the chillies are briefly seared in a pan over medium heat until everything is soft. Add the curry powder and cook a little more.
3. Next to the tomatoes, the broth and the lentils. These are put in the pan and cooked over low heat. About 10 minutes, but the

cooking time depends on how crispy you want the celery.
4. Meanwhile, the salmon is coated with the turmeric, oil and lemon juice. Place the salmon on a tray and bake in the oven for 8-10 minutes.
5. Before serving, mix the parsley with the celery and serve.

Waldorf Salad

Ingredients:

- 1 tablespoon of cold-pressed olive oil
- 1 teaspoon balsamic vinegar
- Juice of ¼ lemon
- A little Dijon mustard
- 50g rocket
- 100g celery green or tuber, roughly chopped
- 50g apple, roughly chopped
- 50g walnuts, roughly chopped
- 10g red onions, roughly chopped

- 5g parsley, finely chopped

- 1 tbsp capers

- 35g chicory

Directions:

1. First we need to mix the celery, apple, walnuts, onions, capers, parsley and lovage in a large bowl.
2. Then we get to the dressing. To do this, we mix the olive oil, the balsamic vinegar, the lemon juice and a little of the Dijon mustard depending on your taste in a measuring cup. We then marinate the finished salad with the dressing.
3. Now it goes to serving. To do this, we arrange the rocket and chicory on a plate and top with the marinated Waldorf salad.

Bacon Roasted Brussel Sprouts

Ingredients:

- 4 cloves garlic, peeled and "smashed"

- 1 cup red potatoes, small diced

- ¼ cup balsamic vinegar

- 2 Tbs Italian parsley minced

- Pinch Kosher salt

- ¼ cup   extra virgin olive oil

- 6 slices Snake River Farms Hardwood Smoked Bacon, cooked, cooled and cut into ¼ inch slices

- 1 lb brussel sprouts, stalk removed, cut in half and then sliced thinly

- Pinch fresh ground black pepper

Directions:

1. Preheat oven to 400 'f. Place heavy roasting pan into oven for 15 mins prior to cooking. Remove heated roasting pan from oven; add a ring of   extra virgin olive oil to pan; add garlic and cooked bacon and mix well.
2. Add potatoes and sprouts, season with salt and pepper. Put into oven and roast for 15-18 mins.
3. Once sprouts are caramelized and potatoes tender, remove from oven and stir in balsamic vinegar.
4. To serve, remove twine and herbs from roast and slice into ¾ inch wide strips.
5. Transfer to serving platter, and surround with roasted sprouts, placing some atop carved

meat. Pour reserve juices over tenderloin, and garnish with fresh parsley.

Maple Roasted Acorn Squash With Cornbread Stuffing

Ingredients:

For the squash

- ½ medium deep green acorn squash, per person
- extra virgin olive oil
- Maple syrup
- Salt, to taste

For the stuffing

- 2 large Granny Smith or other tart apples, peeled, cored and diced
- 1 tsp. thyme, dried

- 1-2 tsp. mild gluten-free curry powder, to taste
- 1/2 tsp. ground cinnamon
- 1 cup fresh chopped cranberries
- 4-5 Tbsp. extra virgin olive oil
- 1 cup diced celery
- 1 cup diced sweet or purple onion
- 1 cup light vegetable broth- more, as needed
- 2 Tbsp. pure maple syrup
- Sea salt and fresh ground pepper, to taste

Directions:

For the squash

1. Preheat oven to 400 F.

2. Carefully slice the acorn squash in half, lengthwise. Clean out the seeds with a spoon.
3. Place the squash in a broiler or roasting pan.
4. If any of the squash is tippy, slice a thin piece off the bottom to make it sit still. Pour some water into the pan you'll need a good inch or two this helps keep the squash from scorching/sticking to the pan.
5. Drizzle the squash with extra virgin olive oil and pure maple syrup until it collects in the hollow. Season with sea salt.
6. Place the pan into the preheated oven. Roast the squash until it is fork tender.

For the stuffing

7. Preheat the oven to 325 degrees F.
8. Heat about 2 Tbsp. of extra virgin olive oil in a large deep skillet; stir in the thyme, curry and cinnamon; add the celery, onion and apples; cook until softened. Remove the

skillet from the burner and set aside to cool a bit.
9. Add in the chopped cranberries. Stir in the toasted cornbread. Mix well. Add a little more extra virgin olive oil, and the broth, pouring in a little at a time and gently stirring to combine.
10. Add the maple syrup. Stir. Season with sea salt and pepper to taste.
11. Some folks like a very soft dressing- if you are one of these, feel free to add more broth.
12. Use for stuffing roasted acorn squash see above for roasting squash. If you happen to be a turkey loving omnivore, grab your spoon and stuff away.
13. Or, bake the stuffing as a side dish in a casserole dish, bake at 350 degrees F till heated through, about 20 to 25 minutes.

Lamb, Butternut Squash And Date Tagine

Ingredients:

- 800g sheep neck filet, cut into 2cm pieces

- ½ teaspoon salt

- 100g Medjool dates, hollowed and hacked

- 400g tin hacked tomatoes, in addition to a large portion of a container of water

- 500g butternut squash, chopped into 1cm 3D shapes

- 400g tin chickpeas, depleted

- 3 tablespoons new coriander in addition to extra for decorate

- 3 tablespoons olive oil

- 2 red onion, cut

- 2cm ginger, ground

- 4 garlic cloves, ground or squashed

- 2 teaspoon stew pieces or to taste

- 3 teaspoons cumin seeds

- 2 cinnamon stick

- 3 teaspoons ground turmeric

- Buckwheat, couscous, flatbreads, or rice to serve

Directions:

1. Preheat your stove to 140C.

2. Drizzle around 3 tablespoons of vegetable oil into a huge ovenproof pot or forged iron meal dish. Include the cut onion and cook on a fragile warmth, with the duvet on, for around 5 minutes, until the onions are mellowed however not dark-colored.
3. Add the bottom garlic and ginger, bean stew, cumin, cinnamon, and turmeric. Mix well and cook for 2 increasingly minute with the duvet off. Include a sprinkle of water if it gets excessively dry.
4. Next, include the sheep pieces. Mix well to hide the meat In the onions and flavors and afterward include the salt, hacked dates, and tomatoes, additionally to a few large portions of a jar of water 100-200ml.
5. Bring the tagine to the bubble and afterward put the duvet on and put in your preheated stove for 1 hour and quarter-hour.

6. Thirty minutes before the finish of the cooking time, include the cleaved butternut squash and depleted chickpeas. Mix everything, set the duvet back on, and are available back to the stove for the last half-hour of cooking.
7. When the tagine is ready, expel from the stove and blend through the cleaved coriander. Present with buckwheat, couscous, flatbreads, or basmati rice.

Prawn Arrabbiata

Ingredients:

- 30 g Celery, finely slashed

- 1 Bird's eye bean stew, finely hacked

- 1 tsp Dried blended herbs

- 1 tsp Extra virgin olive oil

- 2 tbsp White wine discretionary

- 400 g Tinned slashed tomatoes

- 1 tbsp Chopped parsley

- 125-150 g Raw or cooked prawns Ideally ruler prawns

- 65 g Buckwheat pasta

- 1 tbsp Extra virgin olive oil

- For arrabbiata sauce

- 40 g Red onion, finely slashed

- 1 Garlic clove, finely slashed

Directions:

1. Fry the onion, garlic, celery, and bean stew, and dried herbs In the oil over a medium-low warmth for 12 minutes.
2. Turn the warmth up to medium, include the wine, and cook for 2 moment. Include the tomatoes and leave the sauce to stew over a medium-low warmth for 2030 minutes, until it's a pleasing creamy consistency.
3. On the off chance that you simply feel the sauce is getting too thick, just include at least water.
4. While the sauce is cooking, carry a container of water to the bubble and cook the pasta as per the bundle guidelines.
5. At the purpose when prepared even as you'd prefer, channel, hurl with the vegetable oil and confine the container until you've.
6. On the off that you simply are utilizing crude prawns, mix them to the sauce and bake for

an extra 34 minutes until it's turned pink and dark, including the parsley and serve.
7. If you're utilizing cooked prawns, include them with the parsley, carry the sauce to the bubble, and help.
8. Add pasta to the sauce, blend altogether yet tenderly and serve.

Beans With Beef

Ingredients:

- 1 chopped red bell pepper

- 3 finely chopped bird's eye chili peppers
  Canned tomatoes, 800 g

- Ground turmeric, 1 tbsp

- Tomato sauce, 1 tbsp

- Cocoa powder, 1 tbsp

- Ground cumin, 1 tbsp

- Extra virgin olive oil, 1 tbsp

- Red wine, 150 ml

- Kidney beans, 2 small cans

- Lean beef, minced, 400 g

- Buckwheat, 160 g

- 1 finely chopped red onion

- Chopped coriander, ½ tbsp.

- Chopped parsley, ½ tbsp.

Directions:

1. Fry the onions, stew peppers, and garlic for 4 minutes over medium hotness. Toss in the flavors and mince for 2 more moment.
2. From that point onward, add the hamburger and red wine. Heat to the point of boiling and allowed it to rise until the fluid decreases by a half.
3. Add the cocoa powder, tomatoes, pureed tomatoes, and the red ringer pepper. Add

more water if necessary and let the dish stew on low medium hotness for 60 minutes.
4. Add the excess cleaved spices before serving.

Chargrilled Beef, A Red Wine Jus, Onion Rings, Garlic Kale, And Herb Roasted Potatoes

Ingredients:

- 120150g x 3.5cm-thick hamburger filet steak 40ml red wine 150ml meat stock

- 1 teaspoon tomato purée 1 teaspoon corn flour

- 1 tablespoon water

- 5g parsley, finely cleaved

- 50g red onion, cut into rings 50g kale, cut

- 100g potatoes, stripped and dice

- 1 tablespoon extra-virgin olive oil

- 1 garlic clove, finely cleaved

Directions:

1. Preheat the broiler to 220ºC and place the potatoes in bubbling water and cook for 4-5 minutes, channel.
2. Pour 1 teaspoon oil in a stewing tin and dinner the potatoes for 35-45 minutes turning the potatoes on each side predictably to ensure they cook equitably.
3. Remove from the broiler when totally cooked, sprinkle with cut parsley, and mix all together.
4. Pour 1 teaspoon of the oil on a skillet and fry the onion for 5-7 minutes to end up being fragile and advantageously caramelized. Keep it warm.
5. Place the kale in a dish, steam for 2-3 minutes, and channel. In ½ teaspoon of oil, fry the garlic for 1 second to end up being sensitive anyway not t2d.

6. Add the kale and continue to sing for an extra 1-2 minutes to get sensitive. Keep up the glow.
7. Over high warmth, place an ovenproof skillet until it gets smoking.
8. By then use the ½ a teaspoon of the oil to cover the meat and fry over a medium-high warmth. Eliminate the meat and set to the side to rest.
9. Pour the wine to the hot container and air pocket to lessen the wine sum altogether to shape sweet and to taste concentrated. Incorporate the tomato purée and stock to the steak holder and bubble. Incorporate the cornflour glue little without a moment's delay to go probably as a thickener to until the ideal consistency is achieved. Incorporate any juices from the revived steak and present with the kale, onion rings, cooked potatoes, and red wine sauce.

Black Bean Salsa

Ingredients:

- 1 c. salsa
- 6 c. romaine lettuce leaves, torn
- ½ c. avocado, peeled, pitted and cubed
- tbsp. coconut aminos
- ½ tsp. cumin, ground
- 1 c. canned black beans, no-salt-added, drained and rinsed

Directions:

1. In a bowl, combine the beans with the aminos, cumin, salsa, lettuce and avocado,

toss, divide into small bowls and serve as a snack.
2. Enjoy!

Buckwheat Pasta Salad

Ingredients:

- 8 cherry tomatoes,halved
- ½ avocado,diced
- 10 olives
- 1 tbsp extra virgin olive oil
- 50g buckwheat pastacooked according to the packet instructions
- Large handful of rocket
- Small handful of basil leaves
- 20g pine nuts

Directions:

1. Gently combine all the Ingredients: except the pine nuts and arrange on a plate or in a bowl, then scatter the pine nuts over the top.

Greek Salad Skewers

Ingredients:

- 1 yellow pepper, cut into 8 squares

- ½ red onion, cut in half and separated into 8 pieces

- 100g about 10cm cucumber, cut into 4 slices and halved

- 100g feta, cut into 8 cubes

- 2 wooden skewers, soaked in water for 30 minutes

- before use

- 8 large black olives

- 8 cherry tomatoes

For the dressing:

- ½ clove garlic, peeled and crushed
- Few leaves basil, finely chopped or ½ tsp dried mixed herbs to replace basil and oregano
- Few leaves oregano, finely chopped
- Generous seasoning of salt and freshly ground black pepper
- 1 tbsp extra virgin olive oil
- Juice of ½ lemon
- 1 tsp balsamic vinegar

Directions:

1. Thread each skewer with the salad ingredients in the order: olive, tomato, yellow pepper, red onion, cucumber, feta, tomato, olive, yellow pepper, red onion, cucumber, feta.
2. Place all the dressing ingredients in a small bowl and mix together thoroughly. Pour over the skewers.

Mushroom Dip

Ingredients:

- 1 lb. mushrooms, chopped
- 28 oz. tomato sauce, no-salt-added
- Black pepper to the taste
- 1 c. yellow onion, chopped
- 3 garlic cloves, minced

Directions:

1. Put the onion in a pot, add garlic, mushrooms, black pepper and tomato sauce, stir, cook over medium heat for 20 minutes, leave aside to cool down, divide into small bowls and serve.
2. Enjoy!

Choc Chip Granola-Sirtfood Recipes

Ingredients:

- 1 tbsp dark brown sugar
- 2 tbsp rice malt syrup
- 60g good-quality 70%
- dark chocolate chips
- 200g jumbo oats
- 50g pecans, roughly chopped
- 3 tbsp light olive oil 20g butter

Directions:

1. Preheat the oven to 160°C 140°C fan/Gas 3.

2. Line a large baking tray with a silicone sheet or baking parchment.
3. Mix the oats and pecans together in a large bowl. In a small non-stick pan, gently heat the olive oil, butter, brown sugar and rice malt syrup until the butter has melted and the sugar and syrup have dissolved. Do not allow to boil. Pour the syrup over the oats and stir thoroughly until the oats are fully covered.
4. Distribute the granola over the baking tray, spreading right into the corners. Leave clumps of mixture with spacing rather than an even spread. Bake in the oven for 20 minutes until just tinged golden brown at the edges. Remove from the oven and leave to cool on the tray completely.
5. 4 When cool, break up any bigger lumps on the tray with your fingers and then mix in the chocolate chips. Scoop or pour the granola

into an airtight tub or jar. The granola will keep for at least 2 weeks.

Fragrant Asian Hotpot-Sirtfood

Ingredients:

- 1 star anise, crushed or 1/4 tsp ground anise Small handful 10g parsley, stalks finely chopped

- Small handful 1Og coriander, stalks finely chopped

- Juice of 1/2 lime

- 500ml chicken stock, fresh or made with 1 cube

- 1/2 carrot, peeled and cut into matchsticks

- 50g broccoli, cut into small florets

- 50g beansprouts

- 100g raw tiger prawns

- 100g firm tofu, chopped

- 185 calories

- 1 1/2 of you SIRT 5 a day

- 1 tsp tomato purée

- 50g rice noodles, cooked according to packet instructions

- 50g cooked water chestnuts, drained

- 20g sushi ginger, chopped

- 1 tbsp good-quality miso paste

Directions:

1. Place the tomato purée, star anise, parsley stalks, coriander stalks, lime juice and chicken

stock in a large pan and bring to a simmer for 10 minutes.

2. Add the carrot, broccoli, prawns, tofu, noodles and water chestnuts and simmer gently until the prawns are cooked through.
3. Remove from the heat and stir in the sushi ginger and miso paste.
4. Serve sprinkled with the parsley and coriander leaves.

Buckwheat Noodles With Chicken Kale & Miso

Ingredients:

For the noodles:

- 2 brown onion finely diced

- 2 medium free-range chicken breast sliced or diced

- 3 to 4 tablespoons Tamari sauce or soy sauce, for gluten-free

- 4 to Four shiitake mushrooms sliced

- 3 large garlic cloves finely diced

- Five-ounces buckwheat noodles no wheat

- 3 to 4 handfuls of kale leaves stem removed & roughly cut

- 2 long red chilli, thinly sliced seeds in or as desired

- 2 teaspoon of coconut oil or ghee

For the miso dressing:

- 2 teaspoon of sesame oil if desired

- 2 and a half tablespoon fresh organic miso

- 2 tablespoon of lemon or lime juice

- 2 tablespoon of Tamari sauce

- 2 tablespoon of extra-virgin olive oil

Directions:

1. Bring a clean medium saucepan of water to boil.
2. Add the kale and cook for 2 min, until it is slightly wilted. Remove and put aside but

reserve the water andthen bring it back to the boil.

3. Add the soba noodles and then cook according to the package Directions:usually abt five mins. Rinse under cold water and set aside.

4. In the meantime, carefully pan fry the shiitake mushrooms in coconut oil abt 2 teaspoon or a little ghee for 3 to 4 minutes, until lightly browned on all side. Sprinkle with some sea salt and then put aside.

5. In the same frying pan, heat more ghee or coconut oil over medium to high heat. Sauté chilli and onion for 3 to 4 mins and add the chicken pieces afterwards.

6. Cook for five mins over medium heat, stirring a couple of times, then add the tamari sauce, garlic and some water. Cook for an additional 3 to 4 mins, frequently stirring until chicken is well cooked.

7. 4.Lastly, add the soba noodles and kale and then toss through the chicken to heat up.
8. 5.Now mix together the miso dressing and drizzle over the noodles right at the end of cooking and serve to enjoy.

Prawn Stir-Fry With Buckwheat

Ingredients:

- 3 teaspoons of extra virgin olive oil

- 150grams of shelled raw king prawns deveined

- 20grams red onions sliced

- 40grams celery trimmed & sliced

- 5grams of lovage or celery leaves

- 75grams green beans chopped

- 100ml chicken stock

- 3 teaspoons of tamari or soy sauce for gluten-free

- 75grams of soba buckwheat noodles

- 2 garlic clove finely chopped

- 50grams of kale roughly chopped

- 2 bird's eye chilli finely chopped

- 2 teaspoon of fresh ginger finely chopped

Directions:

1. Heat up a clean frying pan over a high heat, and then cook the prawns in 2 teaspoon of the oil and 2 teaspoon of the tamari for 3 to 4 mins. The prawns should be transferred to a plate afterwards. Using a paper towel wipe out the pan, it'll be used again.
2. Proceed to cook the noodles in boiling water for five to eight minutes or according to package Directions:. Remove water and put aside.
3. In the meantime, fry the chilli, garlic, ginger, beans and celery, kale and red onion in the rest of the oil over medium to high heat for 3 to 4 mins. Afterwards, Add the stock and bring to the boil, then simmer for 2 or 3 minutes, until the vegetables are well cooked but sremains crunchy.

4. Add the noodles, lovage or celery leaves and prawns to the pan, bring back to the boil and then remove from the heat. Serve to enjoy.

Buckwheat Groats With Banana And Chocolate Topping

Ingredients:

- 1 map. cinnamon powder
- 3 tsp cocoa powder
- 1 tbsp raw cane sugar
- 125 g buckwheat groats
- 1 banana
- 1 tbsp cocoa nibs
- 400 ml oat drink oat milk
- ½ vanilla bean
- 1 map. ground cardamom

- 1 tsp chia seeds

Directions:

1. Heat the oat drink in a saucepan. Halve the length of the vanilla pod lengthways and scrape out the pulp with a knife. Add the vanilla pulp, the scraped-out vanilla pod, cardamom, cinnamon, cocoa and raw cane sugar to the oat drink, stir and bring to the boil.
2. Stir in the buckwheat, bring to the boil briefly and let it swell for 10 minutes over medium heat, stirring occasionally.
3. Meanwhile, peel the banana and slice the pulp. Heat the butter in a pan and lightly brown the slices of banana over medium heat.
4. Fill buckwheat groats in small bowls and serve garnished with bananas, cocoa nibs, and chia seeds.

Overnight Oats With Banana And Peanut Butter

Ingredients:

- 5 tbsp oatmeal 75 g

- 2 tbsp crushed linseed 15 g

- 200 ml almond drink almond milk

- 2 tbsp peanut butter 30 g

- 1 tsp agave syrup 5 g

- 1 banana

- 1 tbsp salted peanut kernel 15 g

Directions:

1. Mix oatmeal and 1 tablespoon of flax seeds. Add almond milk, 1 tablespoon of peanut butter and agave syrup and stir thoroughly.

Place in the refrigerator for at least 2 hours, preferably overnight.
2. The next morning, peel the banana and cut it into bite-size pieces. Roughly chop peanut kernels as desired.
3. Place overnight oats in 3 small bowls or closable glasses and spread the remaining peanut butter and bananas on top. Sprinkle overnight oats with peanut butter and banana with remaining flaxseed and peanut kernels.

Overnight Oats With Chocolate And Figs

Ingredients:

- 1 tbsp cocoa powder 10 g; heavily oiled

- 200 ml oat drink oat milk

- 2 tbsp pistachio kernels 30 g

- 2nd figs

- 2 stems mint

- 1 pc dark chocolate 30 g; at least 70% cocoa

- 5 tbsp spelled flakes 75 g

- 1 tbsp cocoa nibs 10 g

Directions:

1. Chop chocolate and mix with spelled flakes, cocoa powder and oat milk and put in the fridge for at least 2 hours, better overnight.
2. The next morning, roughly chop the pistachio nuts. Wash the figs, pat dry and quarter them. Wash mint, shake dry and pluck the leaves.
3. Put overnight oats in 3 bowls or closable glasses. Spread figs and mint leaves on top. Sprinkle overnight oats with chocolate and figs with chopped pistachio nuts and cocoa nibs.

Wholesome Buckwheat Granola

Ingredients:

- Ground cardamom half teaspoon
- Date sugar 2 tablespoon
- Olive oil half cup
- Molasses or black treacle half cup
- Chia seeds 2 tablespoon
- Chopped pecans half cup
- Buckwheat groats 2 cup
- Shredded coconuts half cup
- A pinch of sea salt

Directions:

1. Preheat your oven to 320 degrees F.
2. Get a medium-sized bowl, & add the shredded coconut, buckwheat groats, coconut sugar, cardamom, pecans, chia seeds, and sea salt. Mix the Ingredients: together.
3. Place a medium saucepan over medium-low heat, then add the olive oil. Once the oil is hot, add the molasses and stir until melted and properly combined.
4. Mix all the Ingredients: together in a bowl, then spread evenly on a lined baking sheet.
5. Place the baking sheet in the oven for about 27 to 30 minutes stir at intervals.

Cinnamon Buckwheat And Walnuts

Ingredients:

- Pure date syrup 3 tablespoons

- Buckwheat groats 2 cup rinsed

- Chopped walnut ¼ cup

- Water 2 cup

- Almond milk 2 cup

- Cinnamon 2 teaspoon

Directions:

1. Place a saucepan over medium heat, add the water, buckwheat, and almond milk. Allow the mixture to boil, and turn down the heat to

low. Cover your pot and simmer for fifteen minutes.
2. Turn off the heat, leave the pot covered for five minutes, and then add the date syrups, walnuts, and cinnamon. Stir and serve warm.

Nutritional Value per Serving

Pancakes With Apples And Blackcurrants

Ingredients:

- 2 tbsp. raw sugar, coconut sugar, or 2 tbsp. h2y that is warm and easy to distribute

- 2 egg whites

- 1 ¼ cups of milk or soy/rice/coconut

- 2 tsp. extra virgin olive oil

- A dash of salt

- 2 apples, cut into small chunks

- 2 cups of quick cooking oats

- 1 cup flour of your choice

- 1 tsp. baking powder

For the berry topping:

- 1 cup blackcurrants, washed and stalks removed

- 3 tbsp. water

- 2 tbsp. sugar

Directions:

1. Place the Ingredients: for the topping in a small pot simmer, stirring frequently for about 10 minutes until it cooks down and the juices are released.
2. Take the dry Ingredients: and mix in a bowl.
3. After, add the apples and the milk a bit at a time you may not use it all, until it is a batter.
4. Stiffly whisk the egg whites and then gently mix them into the pancake batter.
5. Set aside in the refrigerator. Pour a 2 quarter of the oil onto a flat pan or flat griddle, and when hot, pour some of the batter into it in a pancake shape.
6. When the pancakes start to have golden brown edges and form air bubbles, they may be ready to be gently flipped.
7. Test to be sure the bottom can life away from the pan before actually flipping.
8. Repeat for the next 4 pancakes.

9. Top each pancake with the berries.

Granola

Ingredients:

- 1 cup of cacao nibs or very dark chocolate chips

- 1/2 cup walnuts, chopped

- 1 cup strawberries, chopped and without stems 1 cup plain Greek, or coconut or soy yogurt.

- 1 cup buckwheat puffs

- 1 cup buckwheat flakes ready to eat type, but not whole buckwheat that needs to be cooked ½ cup coconut flakes

- ½ cup Medjool dates, without pits, chopped into smaller, bite-sized pieces

Directions:

1. Mix, without yogurt and strawberry toppings.
2. You can store for up to a week. Store in an airtight container.
3. Add toppings even different berries or different yogurt.
4. You can even use the berry toppings as you will learn how to make from other recipes.

Tuscan Bean Stew

Ingredients:

- 1 x 14 ounce tin slashed Italian tomatoes
- 0.166 ounce tomato purée
- 0.5 ounce tinned blended beans
- 0.5 ounce kale, generally chopped
- 0.5 ounce generally slashed parsley
- 1.41 ounce buckwheat
- 0.5 ounce additional virgin olive oil
- 0.4 ounce red onion, finely chopped
- 1.05 ounce carrot, stripped and finely chopped

- 1.05 ounce celery, managed and finely cleaved

- 2 garlic clove, finely chopped

- ½ 10,000 foot stew, finely hacked optional

- 0.166 ounce herbes de Provence

- ounce vegetable stock

Directions:

1. Put the oil over low to medium hotness in a medium pot and fry the onion, carrot, celery, garlic, bean stew, and spices tenderly until the onion is delicate however not colored.
2. Stir in stock, tomatoes, and purée tomatoes and convey to bubble. Append the beans and need to cook for 30 minutes.

3. Cook for another 5‑10 minutes in the wake of adding kale, then, at that point, add the parsley until tender.
4. Meanwhile, cook the buckwheat as educated by the bundle, channel and afterward present with stew.

Kale And Red Onion Dhal With Buckwheat

Ingredients:

- 2 teaspoons garam masala

- 5.64 ounce red lentils

- 400ml coconut milk

- 6.76 ounce water

- 2 10,000 foot bean stew, deseeded and finely chopped

- 3.52 ounce kale spinach can likewise be used

- 5.64 ounce buckwheat or brown rice

- 0.5 ounce olive oil

- 2 little red onion, sliced

- 4 garlic cloves, ground or squashed 2 cm ginger, grated

- 2 teaspoons turmeric

Directions:

1. In a major, profound pot, place the olive oil and add the cut onion. Cook at low strain, with the cover on until mellowed for 5 minutes.
2. Add the garlic, Chili, and ginger and cook for 1 minute.
3. Add the turmeric, garam masala, sprinkle with water, and cook for 1 minute.
4. Add the red lentils, coconut milk, and 200 ml of water essentially fill the coconut milk with water and tap it into the casserole.

Char Grilled Beef With Onion Rings, Garlic Kale And Herb Roasted Potatoes.

Ingredients:

- 1.76 ounce kale, sliced

- 2 garlic clove, finely chopped

- 5-ounce 3.5cm-thick meat filet steak or 2cm-thick sirloin steak

- Add 40ml red wine

- Add 150ml hamburger stock

- Add 0.166 ounce tomato purée

- Add 0.166 ounce cornflour, broke up in 0.5 ounce water

- 3.5-ounce potatoes, stripped and cut into 2cm dice

- 0.5 ounce additional virgin olive oil

- 0.17 ounce parsley, finely chopped

- 1.76 ounce red onion, cut into rings

Directions:

1. The stove warms up to 430°F.
2. Place the potatoes in a boiling water saucepan, bring it back to the boil and cook for 45 minutes, then drain.
3. Put 0.166 ounce of oil in a broiling tin and fry thirty minutes in a hot broiler. Turn the potatoes after like clockwork to guarantee that they cook uniformly.
4. Eliminate from broiler when cooked, sprinkle with the cleaved parsley and blend well.

5. Fry the onion 57 minutes over medium hotness in 1 teaspoon of oil until delicate and delightfully caramelized. Keep dry. Steam the kale, then steam for 23 minutes. In 1/2 teaspoon of oil, fry the garlic tenderly for 1 moment, until delicate yet not shaded. Add the kale and fry, until delicate, for another 12 minutes. Keep dry.
6. Heat a skillet, which is ovenproof over high hotness until it smokes. Cover the meat in 1/2 teaspoon of the oil and fry over medium-high hotness in the hot skillet, contingent upon how you like your meat cooked.
7. On the off chance that you need your meat medium, it would be simpler to burn the meat and afterward move the container to a 430°F stove and finish the cooking as per the recommended times.
8. Remove the meat from the pan and set to the side for rest.

9. Add the wine to the hot pan to deliver any meat buildup—air pocket to divide the alcohol, to sweet, and with a solid flavor.
10. Transfer the stock and tomato purée to the steak pan and bring to the boiling point, then add the cornflour paste to thicken your sauce, add it a little at a time until the texture you want has been achieved. Connect a portion of the excess steak squeezes and eat with the simmered potatoes, spinach, onion rings, and red wine sauce.
11. Thoroughly combine everything as 2 and cook over a delicate hotness for 20 minutes with the top on.
12. At the point when the dhal begins staying, blend routinely, and apply somewhat more water.
13. Add the kale After 20 minutes, mix completely and substitute the top and cook

for an additional 5 minutes 1-2 minutes in the event that spinach is utilized instead!

Scramble Mushroom And Tofu

Ingredients:

- 1 cup of extra virgin olive oil
- 1/8 cup 20 g red, thinly sliced onion
- 1/2 Thai Chili, with thin slices
- Mushrooms: 3/4 cup 50 g, thinly sliced
- 3 1/2 ounces 100 g of tofu extra firm
- 1 Teaspoon of turmeric powder
- 1 cup of mild curry powder
- 1/3 cup 20 g kale, chopped roughly
- 2 Table cubits 5 g of parsley, finely chopped

Directions:

1. Wrap the tofu in paper towels and top with something heavy to help drain it.
2. Mix the curry and turmeric powder, then add a little water until a light paste has been achieved. Steam the Kale for 3 or 4 minutes.
3. Heat the oil over medium heat in a frying pan and fry the onion, chili and mushrooms for 2 to 3 minutes until browning and softening has begun.
4. Crumble the tofu into pieces of bite size and add to the saucepan, pour over the tofu the spice mix and thoroughly mix.
5. Cook for 2 to 3 minutes over medium heat so that the spices are cooked through and the tofu has begun browning.
6. Add the kale, and continue cooking for another minute over medium heat. Add the parsley, mix well and serve.

Salmon Pasta Smoked With Chili And Arugula

Ingredients:

- Buckwheat pasta: 9 to 11 ounces 250 to 300 g

- 9 Ounces Smoked Salmon 250 g

- 2 Capers spoons

- 1/2 lemon juice

- 2 Ounces Arugula 60 g

- 1/4 cup 10 g chopped parsley

- 2 Spoonfuls of extra virgin olive oil

- 1 Red, finely chopped onion

- 2 Cloves of garlic, finely chopped

- 2 Thai, finely chopped chilies

- 1 cup 150 g of cherry tomatoes, cut in half

- 1/2 cup white wine 100ml

Directions:

1. In a frying pan flame 1 tablespoon of the oil over low heat. Stir in the onion, garlic, chili and fry until soft but not brown.
2. Add the tomatoes and allow to cook for 2 or 3 minutes. To that by half add the white wine and bubble.
3. Cook the pasta in boiling water with 1 tablespoon of oil for 8 to 10 minutes depending on whether you like it al dente, then rinse.
4. Slice the salmon into strips and add the capers, lemon juice, arugula and parsley to the tomato saucepan. Add the pasta, mix well

and serve straight away. Drizzle any oil left over top.

Soba Noodles In Miso Broth With Tofu, Celery And Kale

Ingredients:

- 30g miso paste

- 50g kale, roughly chopped

- 50g celery stalk, roughly chopped

- 1 teaspoon sesame seeds

- 100g tofu, natural, cut into cubes

- 1 tbsp tamari or soy sauce.

- 75g soba noodles

- 1 tbsp olive oil, cold pressed

- 20g red onion, finely sliced

- 1 clove of garlic, finely chopped

- 1 teaspoon of finely chopped ginger

- 300ml vegetable stock

Directions:

1. Let's start with the pasta first. We cook them exactly as it says on the package instructions.
2. While the pasta is cooking, let's do the rest. The onion, garlic and ginger are sautéed in a pan with oil.
3. When that's d2, we add the broth and miso paste to the pan and bring everything to a simmer.
4. Add the cabbage and celery to the simmering Ingredients: and heat for about 5 minutes at a low temperature.
5. Finally, add the noodles, sesame seeds and tofu to the pan to warm up. Season with the soy sauce and serve.

Tuscan-Style Bean Stew

Ingredients:

- 1 can of finely chopped tomatoes 400ml

- 200g canned mixed beans

- 50g kale, roughly chopped up

- 1 tablespoon of coarsely chopped parsley

- 40g buckwheat

- 1 tablespoon of cold-pressed olive oil

- 50g red onion, finely chopped

- 30g carrots, cut into small pieces

- 1 clove of garlic, very finely chopped

- ½ Thai chilli, finely chopped

- 1 teaspoon mixed Italian herbs

- 1 tbsp tomato paste

- 200ml vegetable stock

Directions:

1. To start, heat the oil in a saucepan over a low temperature. Now add onion, carrots, celery, garlic, chilli and herbs. Let it sweat briefly.
2. Now add the broth, tomatoes, tomato paste and beans to the pot. Let everything simmer gently for about 30 minutes.
3. In the meantime, we can prepare the buckwheat.
4. When the beans are well cooked, add the cabbage and cook for another 5 minutes.
5. Refine with the parsley before serving.

Turmeric Baked Salmon

Ingredients:

- 40 g Red onion, finely slashed

- 60 g Tinned green lentils

- 1 Garlic clove, finely slashed

- 1 cm fresh ginger, finely slashed

- 1 Bier's eye bean stew, finely slashed

- 150 g Celery, cut into 2cm lengths

- 1 tsp Mild curry powder

- 130 g Tomato, cut into eight wedges

- 125-150 g Skinned Salmon

- 1 tsp Extra virgin olive oil

- 1 tsp ground turmeric

- 1/4 Juice of a lemon

- For the fiery celery

- 1 tsp Extra virgin olive oil

- 100 ml Chicken or vegetable stock

- 1 tbsp Chopped parsley

Directions:

1. Heat the grill to 200C/gas mark 6.
2. Start with the fiery celery. Warmth a skillet over medium-low heat, include the vegetable oil, at that time the onion, garlic, ginger, bean stew, and celery.

3. Fry tenderly for 23 minutes or until mollified; however, not hued, at that time, include the flavorer and cook for an extra moment.
4. Add the red tomato, then the stock and lentils, and stew delicately for 10 minutes. You would possibly get to increment or decrease the cooking time contingent upon how crunchy you wish your celery.
5. Meanwhile, blend the turmeric, oil, and lemon, squeeze and rub over the salmon.
6. Place on a heating plate and cook for 810 minutes.
7. To complete, mix the parsley through the celery and present it with the salmon.

Buckwheat With Mushrooms And Green Onions

Ingredients:

- 1 cup mushrooms, sliced
- Salt and pepper to taste
- 2 teaspoons butter
- 1 cup buckwheat groats
- 2 cups vegetable or chicken broth
- 3 green onions, thinly sliced

Directions:

1. Combine all Ingredients: in your crockpot. Cover and cook on low for 4 to 4 1/2 hours.

Turmeric Chicken & Kale Salad With H2y Lime Dressing-Sirtfood Recipes

Ingredients:

For the chicken

- 1 teaspoon turmeric powder
- 1 teaspoon lime zest
- juice of ½ lime
- ½ teaspoon salt + pepper
- 1 teaspoon ghee or 1 tbsp coconut oil
- ½ medium brown onion, diced
- 250-300 g / 9 oz. chicken mince or diced up chicken thighs

- 1 large garlic clove, finely diced

For the salad

- 3 large kale leaves, stems removed and chopped ½ avocado, sliced
- handful of fresh coriander leaves, chopped
- handful of fresh parsley leaves, chopped
- 6 broccolini stalks or 2 cups of broccoli florets
- 2 tablespoons pumpkin seeds pepitas

For the dressing

- 3 tablespoons extra-virgin olive oil
- 1 teaspoon raw h2y
- ½ teaspoon wholegrain or Dijon mustard ½ teaspoon sea salt and pepper

- 3 tablespoons lime juice

- 1 small garlic clove, finely diced or grated

Directions:

1. Heat the ghee or coconut oil in a little skillet over medium-high hotness.
2. Add the onion and sauté on medium hotness for 4-5 minutes, until brilliant.
3. Add the chicken mince and garlic and mix for 2-3 minutes over medium-high hotness, breaking it apart.
4. Add the turmeric, lime zing, lime squeeze, salt and pepper and cook, blending every now and again, for a further 3-4 minutes. Set the cooked mince aside.
5. While the chicken is cooking, carry a little pot of water to bubble.
6. Add the broccolini and cook for 2 minutes. Wash under chilly water and cut into 3-4 pieces each.

7. Add the pumpkin seeds to the skillet from the chicken and toast over medium hotness for 2 minutes, blending oftentimes to forestall consuming.
8. Season with somewhat salt. Put away. Crude pumpkin seeds are likewise fine to use.
9. Place hacked kale in a serving of mixed greens bowl and pour over the dressing.
10. Utilizing your hands, throw and back rub the kale with the dressing.
11. This will relax the kale, similar to how citrus juice fishes or hamburger carpaccio - it 'cooks' it slightly.
12. Finally toss through the cooked chicken, broccolini, fresh herbs, pumpkin seeds and avocado slices.

Chicken Breasts

Ingredients:

- 120 g skinless, b2less chicken breast 3 tsp. ground Tumeric juice of 1/4 lemon 2 tbsp. extra virgin olive oil

- 50 g kale, chopped

- Twenty g red onion, chopped

- 2 tsp. fresh ginger

- 50 g buckwheat

For the Salsa:

- 130 g tomato

- 2 bird's eye chili, finely chopped

- 2 tbsp. capers, finely chopped

- Five g parsley, finely chopped juice of 1/4 lemon

Directions:

1. To make the salsa, eliminate the eye from the tomato and cleave it finely, taking consideration to keep however much of the fluid as could be expected.
2. Blend in with the stew, tricks, parsley, and lemon juice. You could place everything in a blender however the outcome is a little different.
3. Heat the stove to 220ºC/gas 7. Marinate the chicken bosom in 1 teaspoon of turmeric, lemon juice, and a little oil. Leave for 5-10 minutes.
4. Heat an ovenproof skillet until hot, then, at that point, add the marinated chicken and cook briefly or so on each side, until pale

brilliant, then, at that point, move to the broiler put on a baking plate on the off chance that your dish isn't ovenproof for 8-10 minutes or until cooked through.

5. Eliminate from the broiler, cover with foil, and pass on to rest for 5 minutes before serving.
6. Meanwhile, cook the kale in a liner for 5 minutes. Fry the red onions and the ginger in a little oil, until delicate however not shaded, then, at that point, add the cooked kale and fry for another minute.
7. Cook the buckwheat as indicated by the parcel Directions:with the excess teaspoon of turmeric. Serve close by the chicken, vegetables, and salsa.

Sweet Potato Breakfast

Ingredients:

- ¼ cup fat-free coconut Greek yogurt
- 1/8 cup unsweetened toasted coconut flakes
- 1 chopped apple
- 1 tablespoon maple syrup
- Potatoes

Directions:

1. Preheat oven to 400ºF.
2. Place your potatoes on a baking sheet.
3. Bake them for 4560 minutes or until soft.
4. Use a sharp knife to mark "X" on the potatoes and fluff pulp with a fork.

5. Top with coconut flakes, chopped apple, Greek yogurt, and maple syrup.
6. Serve immediately.

French Toast With Apple Sauce

Ingredients:

- 2 eggs

- 6 slices whole-wheat bread

- 1 teaspoon ground cinnamon

- ¼ cup unsweetened applesauce

- ½ cup skim milk

- 2 packets of Stevia

Directions:

1. Mix well applesauce, sugar, cinnamon, milk, and eggs in a mixing bowl.
2. 2 slice at a time, soak the bread into an applesauce mixture until wet.

3. On medium fire, heat a large nonstick skillet.
4. Add soaked bread on 2 side and another on the other side. Cook in a single layer in batches for 23 minutes per side on medium-low fire or until lightly browned.
5. Serve and enjoy.

Veggie Omelet

Ingredients:

- 1 bird's eye chili, diced
- A small handful of kale, chopped
- A small handful of arugula, chopped
- 4 eggs
- 2 tablespoons olive oil to cook
- 1 small onion, chopped

Directions:

1. Heat olive oil in a frying pan at medium-high heat

2. Cook the onions with the pepper until fragrant and the onions begin to turn translucent.
3. Then, add in the chopped greens. Wait for them to wilt. Then, remove from the pan into a small bowl.
4. Crack eggs into a separate bowl and beat until mixed and combined.
5. Salt and pepper to taste and then add the eggs to the frying pan, careful to spread them evenly.
6. After a minute of cooking, as the bottom of the egg starts to firm up, add the veggie mixture to the pan and spread them out on 2 half of the omelet.
7. Then, fold the egg over the veggies. Slide onto a plate, cut in half, and serve.

Main Meals Recipe

Ingredients:

- 2 red onions, chopped

- 2 tablespoons plain flour

- 2 tablespoons olive oil

- 1¼ pints red wine

- 1 bouquet grain

- 1 pound button mushrooms

- 3½ ounces streaky bacon, chopped

- 16 chicken thighs, skin removed

- 3 cloves of garlic, crushed

- 3 tablespoons fresh parsley, chopped

- 3 carrots, chopped

Directions:

1. In a large plate, put the flour and coat the chicken in it. Heat the olive oil then add the chicken and brown it, before setting aside.
2. Fry the bacon in the pan then add the onion and cook for 5 minutes. Pour in the red wine and add the chicken, carrots, bouquet grain and garlic.
3. Transfer it to a large ovenproof dish. Cook at 180C/360F for an hour.
4. Remove the bouquet grain and skim off any excess fat, if necessary. Add in the mushrooms and cook for 15 minutes. Stir in the parsley just before serving.

Salmon & Capers

Ingredients:

- 1 tablespoon capers, chopped
- 2 teaspoons fresh parsley
- Zest of 1 lemon
- 3 ounces Greek yogurt
- 4 salmon fillets, skin removed
- 4 teaspoons Dijon Mustard

Directions:

1. Put the yogurt, mustard, lemon zest, parsley and capers in a mixing bowl. Thoroughly coat the salmon in the mixture.

2. Place the salmon under a hot grill broiler and cook for 3-4 minutes on each side, or until the fish is cooked.
3. Serve with mashed potatoes and vegetables or a large green leafy salad.

Moroccan Chicken Casserole

Ingredients:

- 1 teaspoon ground cinnamon
- 1 teaspoon ground turmeric
- 1 bird's-eye chili, chopped
- 1 pints chicken stock broth
- 1 ounce corn flour
- 2fl ounces water
- 2 tablespoons fresh coriander
- 9 ounces tinned chickpeas garbanzo beans drained

- 4 chicken breasts, cubed

- 4 Medrol dates, halved

- 6 dried apricots, halved

- 1 red onion, sliced

- 1 carrot, chopped

- 1 teaspoon ground cumin

Directions:

1. Place the chicken, chickpeas garbanzo beans, onion, carrot, chili, cumin, turmeric, cinnamon and stock broth into a large saucepan.
2. Put it to the boil, and reduce heat after that simmer for 25 minutes. Add in the dates and apricots and simmer for 10 minutes.
3. In a cup, mix the corn flour together with the water until it becomes a smooth paste.

4. Pour the mixture into the saucepan and stir until it thickens.
5. Add in the coriander cilantro and mix well. Serve with buckwheat or couscous.

Sesame Dip

Ingredients:

- ½ c. lemon juice
- ½ tsp. cumin, ground
- 3 garlic cloves, chopped
- 1 c. sesame seed paste, pure
- Black pepper to the taste
- 1 c. veggie stock

Directions:

1. In your food processor, mix the sesame paste with black pepper, stock, lemon juice, cumin and garlic, pulse very well, divide into bowls and serve as a party dip. Enjoy!

Salsa Bean Dip

Ingredients:

- 1 c. low-fat cheddar, shredded
- 2 tbsps. green onions, chopped
- ½ c. salsa
- 2 c. canned white beans, no-salt-added, drained and rinsed

Directions:

1. In a small pot, combine the beans with the green onions and salsa, stir, bring to a simmer over medium heat, cook for 20 minutes, add cheese, stir until it melts, take off heat, leave aside to cool down, divide into bowls and serve. Enjoy!

www.ingramcontent.com/pod-product-compliance
Lightning Source LLC
LaVergne TN
LVHW021239080526
838199LV00088B/4749